APOSTOLIC LETTER

DESIDERIO DESIDERAVI

OF THE HOLY FATHER
FRANCIS

TO THE BISHOPS, PRIESTS AND DEACONS,
TO CONSECRATED MEN AND WOMEN
AND TO THE LAY FAITHFUL

ON THE LITURGICAL FORMATION
OF THE PEOPLE OF GOD

*All documents are published
thanks to the generosity of the supporters
of the Catholic Truth Society*

Cover image: Pope Francis celebrating mass on the Solemnity of the Epiphany 2016 in St Peter's basilica, Rome. © Stefano Spaziani

This edition first published 2022 by The Incorporated Catholic Truth Society 42-46 Harleyford Road London SE11 5AY. www.ctsbooks.org.

Libreria Editrice Vaticana omnia sibi vindicat iura. Sine eiusdem licentia scripto data nemini liceat hunc Desiderio Desideravi denuo imprimere aut in aliam linguam vertere. Copyright © 2022 Libreria Editrice Vaticana 00120 Città del Vaticano. Tel. 06.698.45780 – Fax 06.698.84716 Email: commerciale. lev@spc.va

ISBN 978 1 78469 749 5

CONTENTS

THE LITURGY: THE "TODAY" OF SALVATION HISTORY ... 5

THE LITURGY: PLACE OF ENCOUNTER WITH CHRIST ... 8

THE CHURCH: SACRAMENT OF THE BODY OF CHRIST .. 10

THE THEOLOGICAL SENSE OF THE LITURGY 11

THE LITURGY: ANTIDOTE FOR THE POISON
OF SPIRITUAL WORLDLINESS 12

REDISCOVERING DAILY THE BEAUTY OF THE TRUTH
OF THE CHRISTIAN CELEBRATION 14

AMAZEMENT BEFORE THE PASCHAL MYSTERY:
AN ESSENTIAL PART OF THE LITURGICAL ACT 15

THE NEED FOR A SERIOUS AND VITAL
LITURGICAL FORMATION 16

ARS CELEBRANDI 27

*Desiderio desideravi
hoc Pascha manducare vobiscum,
antequam patiar*

(Lk 22:15)

DESIDERIO DESIDERAVI

1. My dearest brothers and sisters, with this letter I desire to reach you all – after having written already only to the bishops after the publication of the Motu Proprio *Traditionis custodes* – and I write to share with you some reflections on the liturgy, a dimension fundamental for the life of the Church. The theme is vast and always deserves an attentive consideration in every one of its aspects. Even so, with this letter I do not intend to treat the question in an exhaustive way. I simply desire to offer some prompts or cues for reflections that can aid in the contemplation of the beauty and truth of Christian celebration.

The Liturgy: the "today" of salvation history

2. *"I have earnestly desired to eat this Passover with you before I suffer."* (*Lk* 22:15) These words of Jesus, with which the account of the Last Supper opens, are the crevice through which we are given the surprising possibility of intuiting the depth of the love of the persons of the Most Holy Trinity for us.

3. Peter and John were sent to make preparations to eat that Passover, but in actual fact, all of creation, all of history – which at last was on the verge of revealing itself as the history of salvation – was a huge preparation for that Supper. Peter and the others are present at that table, unaware and yet necessary. Necessary because every gift, to be gift, must have someone disposed to receive it. In this case, the disproportion between the immensity of the gift and the smallness of the one who receives it is infinite, and it cannot fail to surprise us. Nonetheless, through the mercy of the Lord, the gift is entrusted to the Apostles so that it might be carried to every man and woman.

4. No one had earned a place at that Supper. All had been invited. Or better said: all had been drawn there by the burning desire that Jesus had to eat that Passover with them. He knows that he is the Lamb of that Passover meal; he knows that he *is* the Passover. This is the absolute newness, the absolute originality, of that Supper, the only truly new thing in history, which renders that Supper unique and for this reason "the Last Supper," unrepeatable. Nonetheless, his infinite desire to re-establish that communion with us that was and remains his original design, will not be satisfied until every man and woman, *from every tribe, tongue, people and nation* (*Rv* 5:9), shall have eaten his Body and drunk his Blood. And for this reason that same Supper will be made present in the celebration of the Eucharist until he returns again.

5. The world still does not know it, but everyone is *invited to the supper of the wedding of the Lamb* (*Rv* 19:9). To be admitted to the feast all that is required is the wedding garment of faith which comes from the hearing of his Word (cf. *Rm* 10:17). The Church tailors such a garment to fit each one with the whiteness of a garment *bathed in the blood of the Lamb.* (*Rv* 7:14). We must not allow ourselves even a moment of rest, knowing that still not everyone has received an invitation to this Supper or knowing that others have forgotten it or have got lost along the way in the twists and turns of human living. This is what I spoke of when I said, "I dream of a 'missionary option', that is, a missionary impulse capable of transforming everything, so that the Church's customs, ways of doing things, times and schedules, language and structures can be suitably channelled for the evangelisation of today's world rather than for her self-preservation." (*Evangelii gaudium*, n. 27). I want this so that all can be seated at the Supper of the sacrifice of the Lamb and live from him.

6. Before our response to his invitation – well before! – there is his desire for us. We may not even be aware of it, but every time we go to Mass, the first reason is that we are drawn there by his desire for us. For our part, the possible response – which is also the most demanding asceticism – is, as always, that surrender to this love, that letting ourselves be drawn by him. Indeed, every reception of communion of the Body and Blood of Christ was already desired by him in the Last Supper.

7. The content of the bread broken is the cross of Jesus, his sacrifice of obedience out of love for the Father. If we had not had the Last Supper, that is to say, if we had not had the ritual anticipation of his death, we would have never been able to grasp how the carrying out of his being condemned to death could have been in fact *the* act of perfect worship, pleasing to the Father, the only true act of worship, the only true liturgy. Only a few hours after the Supper, the apostles could have seen in the cross of Jesus, if they could have borne the weight of it, what it meant for Jesus to say, "body offered," "blood poured out." It is this of which we make memorial in every Eucharist. When the Risen One returns from the dead to break the bread for the disciples at Emmaus, and for his disciples who had gone back to fishing for fish and not for people on the Sea of Galilee, that gesture of breaking the bread opens their eyes. It heals them from the blindness inflicted by the horror of the cross, and it renders them capable of "seeing" the Risen One, of believing in the Resurrection.

8. If we had somehow arrived in Jerusalem after Pentecost and had felt the desire not only to have information about Jesus of Nazareth but rather the desire still to be able to meet him, we would have had no other possibility than that of searching out his disciples so that we could hear his words and see his gestures, more alive than ever. We would have had no other

possibility of a true encounter with him other than that of the community that celebrates. For this reason the Church has always protected as its most precious treasure the command of the Lord, "Do this in memory of me."

9. From the very beginning the Church was aware that this was not a question of a representation, however sacred it be, of the Supper of the Lord. It would have made no sense, and no one would have been able to think of "staging" – especially before the eyes of Mary, the Mother of the Lord – that highest moment of the life of the Master. From the very beginning the Church had grasped, enlightened by the Holy Spirit, that that which was visible in Jesus, that which could be seen with the eyes and touched with the hands, his words and his gestures, the concreteness of the incarnate Word – everything of him had passed into the celebration of the sacraments.[1]

The Liturgy: place of encounter with Christ

10. Here lies all the powerful beauty of the liturgy. If the resurrection were for us a concept, an idea, a thought; if the Risen One were for us the recollection of the recollection of others, however authoritative, as, for example, of the Apostles; if there were not given also to us the possibility of a true encounter with him, that would be to declare the newness of the Word made flesh to have been all used up. Instead, the Incarnation, in addition to being the only always new event that history knows, is also the very method that the Holy Trinity has chosen to open to us the way of communion. Christian faith is either an encounter with him alive, or it does not exist.

---

[1] Cf. Leo Magnus, *Sermo LXXIV: De ascensione Domini II, 1*: *quod [...] Redemptoris nostri conspicuum fuit, in sacramenta transivit*".

11. The Liturgy guarantees for us the possibility of such an encounter. For us a vague memory of the Last Supper would do no good. We need to be present at that Supper, to be able to hear his voice, to eat his Body and to drink his Blood. We need him. In the Eucharist and in all the sacraments we are guaranteed the possibility of encountering the Lord Jesus and of having the power of his Paschal Mystery reach us. The salvific power of the sacrifice of Jesus, his every word, his every gesture, glance, and feeling reaches us through the celebration of the sacraments. I am Nicodemus, the Samaritan woman at the well, the man possessed by demons at Capernaum, the paralytic in the house of Peter, the sinful woman pardoned, the woman afflicted by haemorrhages, the daughter of Jairus, the blind man of Jericho, Zacchaeus, Lazarus, the thief and Peter both pardoned. The Lord Jesus who dies no more, who lives forever with the signs of his Passion[2] continues to pardon us, to heal us, to save us with the power of the sacraments. It is the concrete way, by means of his Incarnation, that he loves us. It is the way in which he satisfies his own thirst for us that he had declared from the cross (*Jn* 19:28).

12. Our first encounter with his paschal deed is the event that marks the life of all believers: our Baptism. This is not a mental adhesion to his thought or the agreeing to a code of conduct imposed by him. Rather, it is a being plunged into his passion, death, resurrection and ascension, a being plunged into his paschal deed. It is not magic. Magic is the opposite of the logic of the sacraments because magic pretends to have a power over God, and for this reason it comes from the Tempter. In perfect continuity with the Incarnation, there is given to us, in virtue of the presence and action of the Spirit, the possibility of dying and rising in Christ.

---

[2] *Præfatio paschalis III, Missale Romanum* (2008) p. 367: "*Qui immolátus iam non móritur, sed semper vivit occísus*".

13. How moving, the way in which this comes about. The prayer for the blessing of baptismal water[3] reveals to us that God created water precisely with Baptism in mind. This means that when God created water, he was thinking of the Baptism of each one of us, and this same thought accompanied him all throughout his acting in the history of salvation every time that, with precise intention, he used water for his saving work. It is as if after having created water in the first place, he had wanted to perfect it by making it eventually to be the water of Baptism. It was thus that he wanted to fill it with the movement of his Spirit hovering over the face of the waters (*Gn* 1:2) so that it could contain hidden within the power to sanctify. He used water to regenerate humanity through the flood (*Gn* 6:1-9,29). He controlled it, separating it to open the way of freedom through the Red Sea (cf. *Ex* 14). He consecrated it in the Jordan, plunging into it the flesh of the Word soaked in the Spirit (cf. *Mt* 3:13-17; *Mk* 1:9-11; *Lk* 3:21-22). At the end he blended it with the blood of his Son, the gift of the Spirit inseparably united with the gift of the life and death of the Lamb slain for us, and from his pierced side he poured it out over us (*Jn* 19:34). And it is into this water that we have been immersed so that through its power we can be inserted into the Body of Christ and with him rise to immortal life (cf. *Rm* 6:1-11).

The Church: Sacrament of the Body of Christ

14. As the Second Vatican Council reminded us (cf. *Sacrosanctum Concilium*, n. 5), citing the scriptures, the Fathers, and the Liturgy – the pillars of authentic Tradition – *it was from the side of Christ as he slept the sleep of death upon the cross that there came forth "the wondrous sacrament of the whole Church."*[4] The parallel between the first Adam and

---

[3] Cf. *Missale Romanum* (2008) p. 532.

[4] Cf. Augustinus, *Enarrationes in psalmos. Ps. 138,2; Oratio post septimam lectionem, Vigilia paschalis, Missale Romanum* (2008) p. 359; *Super oblata, Pro Ecclesia* (B), *Missale Romanum* (2008) p. 1076.

the new Adam is striking: as from the side of the first Adam, after having cast him into a deep sleep, God draws forth Eve, so also from the side of the new Adam, sleeping the sleep of death on the cross, there is born the new Eve, the Church. The astonishment for us lies in the words that we can imagine the new Adam made his own in gazing at the Church: "Here at last is bone of my bones and flesh of my flesh" (*Gn* 2:23). For our having believed in his Word and descended into the waters of Baptism, we have become bone of his bone and flesh of his flesh.

15. Without this incorporation there is no possibility of living the fulness of the worship of God. In fact, there is only one act of worship, perfect and pleasing to the Father; namely, the obedience of the Son, the measure of which is his death on the cross. The only possibility of being able to participate in his offering is by becoming "sons in the Son." This is the gift that we have received. The subject acting in the Liturgy is always and only Christ-Church, the mystical Body of Christ.

The theological sense of the Liturgy

16. We owe to the Council – and to the liturgical movement that preceded it – the rediscovery of a theological understanding of the Liturgy and of its importance in the life of the Church. As the general principles spelt out in *Sacrosanctum Concilium* have been fundamental for the reform of the liturgy, they continue to be fundamental for the promotion of that full, conscious, active and fruitful celebration (cf. *Sacrosanctum Concilium*, nn. 11; 14) in the liturgy, "the primary and indispensable source from which the faithful are to derive the true Christian spirit" (*Sacrosanctum Concilium*, n. 14). With this letter I simply want to invite the whole Church to rediscover, to safeguard, and to live the truth and power of the Christian celebration. I want the beauty of the Christian celebration and its necessary consequences for the life of the Church not to be spoiled by

a superficial and foreshortened understanding of its value or, worse yet, by its being exploited in service of some ideological vision, no matter what the hue. The priestly prayer of Jesus at the Last Supper that all may be one (*Jn* 17:21) judges every one of our divisions around the Bread broken, around *the sacrament of mercy, the sign of unity, the bond of charity*.[5]

The Liturgy: antidote for the poison of spiritual worldliness

17. On different occasions I have warned against a dangerous temptation for the life of the Church, which I called "spiritual worldliness." I spoke about this at length in the exhortation *Evangelii gaudium* (nn. 93-97), pinpointing Gnosticism and neo-Pelagianism as two versions connected between themselves that feed this spiritual worldliness.

The first shrinks Christian faith into a subjectivism that "ultimately keeps one imprisoned in his or her own thoughts and feelings." (EG 94) The second cancels out the role of grace and "leads instead to a narcissistic and authoritarian elitism, whereby instead of evangelising, one analyses and classifies others, and instead of opening the door to grace, one exhausts his or her energies in inspecting and verifying." (EG 94)

These distorted forms of Christianity can have disastrous consequences for the life of the Church.

18. From what I have recalled above it is clear that the Liturgy is, by its very nature, the most effective antidote against these poisons. Obviously, I am speaking of the Liturgy in its theological sense and certainly not, as Pius XII already affirmed, Liturgy as *decorative ceremonies or a mere sum total of laws and precepts that govern the cult*.[6]

---

[5] Cf. Augustinus, *In Ioannis Evangelium tractatus XXVI, 13*.
[6] Cf. Litteræ encyclicæ *Mediator Dei* (20th Novembris 1947) in *AAS* 39 (1947) 532.

19. If Gnosticism intoxicates us with the poison of subjectivism, the liturgical celebration frees us from the prison of a self-referencing nourished by one's own reasoning and one's own feeling. The action of the celebration does not belong to the individual but to the Christ-Church, to the totality of the faithful united in Christ. The liturgy does not say "I" but "we," and any limitation on the breadth of this "we" is always demonic. The Liturgy does not leave us alone to search out an individual supposed knowledge of the mystery of God. Rather, it takes us by the hand, together, as an assembly, to lead us deep within the mystery that the Word and the sacramental signs reveal to us. And it does this, consistent with all action of God, following the way of the Incarnation, that is, by means of the symbolic language of the body, which extends to things in space and time.

20. If neo-Pelagianism intoxicates us with the presumption of a salvation earned through our own efforts, the liturgical celebration purifies us, proclaiming the gratuity of the gift of salvation received in faith. Participating in the Eucharistic sacrifice is not our own achievement, as if because of it we could boast before God or before our brothers and sisters. The beginning of every celebration reminds me who I am, asking me to confess my sin and inviting me to implore the Blessed Mary ever-Virgin, the angels and saints and all my brothers and sisters to pray for me to the Lord our God. Certainly, we are not worthy to enter his house; we need a word of his to be saved (cf. *Mt* 8:8). We have no other boast but the cross of our Lord Jesus Christ (cf. *Gal* 6:14). The Liturgy has nothing to do with an ascetical moralism. It is the gift of the Paschal Mystery of the Lord which, received with docility, makes our life new. The cenacle is not entered except through the power of attraction of his desire to eat the Passover with us: *Desiderio desideravi hoc Pascha manducare vobiscum, antequam patiar* (*Lk* 22:15).

*Rediscovering daily the beauty of the truth
of the Christian celebration*

21. But we must be careful: for the antidote of the Liturgy to be effective, we are required every day to rediscover the beauty of the truth of the Christian celebration. I refer once again to the theological sense, as n. 7 of *Sacrosanctum Concilium* so beautifully describes it: the Liturgy is the priesthood of Christ, revealed to us and given in his Paschal Mystery, rendered present and active by means of signs addressed to the senses (water, oil, bread, wine, gestures, words), so that the Spirit, plunging us into the Paschal Mystery, might transform every dimension of our life, conforming us more and more to Christ.

22. The continual rediscovery of the beauty of the Liturgy is not the search for a ritual aesthetic which is content with only a careful exterior observance of a rite or is satisfied by a scrupulous observance of the rubrics. Obviously, what I am saying here does not wish in any way to approve the opposite attitude, which confuses simplicity with a careless banality, or what is essential with an ignorant superficiality, or the concreteness of ritual action with an exasperating practical functionalism.

23. Let us be clear here: every aspect of the celebration must be carefully tended to (space, time, gestures, words, objects, vestments, song, music…) and every rubric must be observed. Such attention would be enough to prevent robbing from the assembly what is owed to it; namely, the Paschal Mystery celebrated according to the ritual that the Church sets down. But even if the quality and the proper action of the celebration were guaranteed, that would not be enough to make our participation full.

Amazement before the Paschal Mystery:
an essential part of the liturgical act

24. If there were lacking our astonishment at the fact that the Paschal Mystery is rendered present in the concreteness of sacramental signs, we would truly risk being impermeable to the ocean of grace that floods every celebration. Efforts to favour a greater quality to the celebration, even if praiseworthy, are not enough; nor is the call for a greater interiority. Interiority can run the risk of reducing itself to an empty subjectivity if it has not taken on board the revelation of the Christian mystery. The encounter with God is not the fruit of an individual interior searching for him, but it is an event given. We can encounter God through the new fact of the Incarnation that reaches in the Last Supper the extreme point of his desiring to be eaten by us. How can the misfortune of distancing ourselves from the allure of the beauty of this gift happen to us?

25. When I speak of astonishment at the Paschal Mystery, I do not at all intend to refer to what at times seems to me to be meant by the vague expression "sense of mystery." Sometimes this is among the presumed chief accusations against the liturgical reform. It is said that the sense of mystery has been removed from the celebration. The astonishment or wonder of which I speak is not some sort of being overcome in the face of an obscure reality or a mysterious rite. It is, on the contrary, marvelling at the fact that the salvific plan of God has been revealed in the paschal deed of Jesus (cf. *Eph* 1:3-14), and the power of this paschal deed continues to reach us in the celebration of the "mysteries," of the sacraments. It is still true that the fulness of revelation has, in respect to our human finitude, an abundance that transcends us and will find its fulfilment at the end of time when the Lord will return. But if the astonishment is of the right kind, then there is no risk that the otherness of God's presence will not be perceived, even within the closeness that the Incarnation intends. If the reform

has eliminated that vague "sense of mystery," then more than a cause for accusations, it is to its credit. Beauty, just like truth, always engenders wonder, and when these are referred to the mystery of God, they lead to adoration.

26. Wonder is an essential part of the liturgical act because it is the way that those who know they are engaged in the particularity of symbolic gestures look at things. It is the marvelling of those who experience the power of symbol, which does not consist in referring to some abstract concept but rather in containing and expressing in its very concreteness what it signifies.

The need for a serious and vital liturgical formation

27. Therefore, the fundamental question is this: how do we recover the capacity to live completely the liturgical action? This was the objective of the Council's reform. The challenge is extremely demanding because modern people – not in all cultures to the same degree – have lost the capacity to engage with symbolic action, which is an essential trait of the liturgical act.

28. With post-modernity people feel themselves even more lost, without references of any sort, lacking in values because they have become indifferent, completely orphaned, living a fragmentation in which an horizon of meaning seems impossible. And so it is even more weighed down by the burdensome inheritance that the previous epoch left us, consisting in individualism and subjectivism (which evokes once again the Pelagian and gnostic problems). It consists also in an abstract spiritualism which contradicts human nature itself, for a human person is an incarnate spirit and therefore as such capable of symbolic action and of symbolic understanding.

29. It is with this reality of the modern world that the Church, united in Council, wanted to enter into contact, reaffirming her awareness of being the sacrament of Christ, the Light of the nations (*Lumen gentium*), putting herself in a devout listening to the *Word of God (Dei Verbum),* and recognising as her own *the joys and the hopes (Gaudium et spes)* of the people of our times. The great Constitutions of the Council cannot be separated one from the other, and it is not an accident that this single huge effort at reflection by the Ecumenical Council – which is the highest expression of synodality in the Church and whose richness I, together with all of you, am called to be the custodian – began with reflection on the Liturgy *(Sacrosanctum Concilium).*

30. Closing the second session of the Council (4th December 1963) St Paul VI expressed himself in this way:

> "The difficult, complex debates have had rich results. They have brought one topic to a conclusion, the sacred liturgy. Treated before all others, in a sense it has priority over all others for its intrinsic dignity and importance to the life of the Church and today we will solemnly promulgate the document on the liturgy. Our spirit, therefore, exults with true joy, for in the way things have gone we note respect for a right scale of values and duties. God must hold first place; prayer to him is our first duty. The liturgy is the first source of divine communion in which God shares his own life with us. It is also the first school of the spiritual life. The liturgy is the first gift we must make to the Christian people united to us by faith and the fervour of their prayers. It is also a primary invitation to the human race, so that all may now lift their mute voices in blessed and genuine prayer and thus may experience that indescribable regenerative power to be found when they join us in proclaiming the praises of God and the hopes of the human heart through Jesus Christ and in the Holy Spirit".[7]

---

[7] *AAS* 56 (1964) 34.

31. In this letter I cannot dwell with you on the richness of this passage's various expressions, which I recommend to your own meditation. If the liturgy is "the summit toward which the activity of the Church is directed, and at the same time the font from which all her power flows" (*Sacrosanctum Concilium,* n. 10), well then, we can understand what is at stake in the liturgical question. It would be trivial to read the tensions, unfortunately present around the celebration, as a simple divergence between different tastes concerning a particular ritual form. The problematic is primarily ecclesiological. I do not see how it is possible to say that one recognises the validity of the Council – though it amazes me that a Catholic might presume not to do so – and at the same time not accept the liturgical reform born out of *Sacrosanctum Concilium,* a document that expresses the reality of the Liturgy intimately joined to the vision of Church so admirably described in *Lumen gentium.* For this reason, as I already expressed in my letter to all the bishops, I have felt it my duty to affirm that "The liturgical books promulgated by St Paul VI and St John Paul II, in conformity with the decrees of Vatican Council II, are the unique expression of the *lex orandi* of the Roman Rite." (Motu Proprio *Traditionis custodes,* art. 1)

The non-acceptance of the liturgical reform, as also a superficial understanding of it, distracts us from the obligation of finding responses to the question that I come back to repeating: how can we grow in our capacity to live in full the liturgical action? How do we continue to let ourselves be amazed at what happens in the celebration under our very eyes? We are in need of a serious and dynamic liturgical formation.

32. Let us return to the cenacle in Jerusalem. On the morning of Pentecost the Church is born, the initial cell of the new humanity. Only the community of men and women – reconciled because pardoned, alive because he is alive, true because dwelt in by the Spirit of truth – can open the cramped space of spiritual individualism.

33. It is the community of Pentecost that is able to break the Bread in the certain knowledge that the Lord is alive, risen from the dead, present with his word, with his gestures, with the offering of his Body and his Blood. From that moment on the celebration became the privileged place – though not the only one – of an encounter with him. We know that only thanks to the grace of this encounter does a human being become fully human. Only the Church of Pentecost can conceive of the human being as a person, open to a full relationship with God, with creation, and with one's brothers and sisters.

34. In this is posed the decisive question of liturgical formation. Romano Guardini says, "Here too the first practical task is indicated: carried along by this inner transformation of our time, we must learn anew how to relate religiously as fully human beings."[8] This is what the Liturgy makes possible. For this we must be formed. Guardini does not hesitate to declare that without liturgical formation "then ritual and textual reforms won't help much."[9] I do not intend to treat here in an exhaustive way the very rich theme of liturgical formation. I only want to offer some starting points for reflection. I think two aspects can be distinguished: formation for the Liturgy and formation by the Liturgy. The first depends upon the second which is essential.

35. It was and is necessary to find the channels for a formation that is the study of Liturgy. From the beginning of the liturgical movement much has been done in this regard, with precious contributions from scholars and academic institutions. Nonetheless, it is important now to spread this knowledge beyond the academic environment, in an accessible way, so that each one of the faithful might grow in a knowledge of the theological sense of the Liturgy. This is the decisive question,

---

[8] R. Guardini, *Liturgische Bildung* (1923) in *Liturgie und liturgische Bildung* (Mainz 1992) p. 43.

[9] R. Guardini, *Der Kultakt und die gegenwärtige Aufgabe der Liturgischen Bildung* (1964) in *Liturgie und liturgische Bildung* (Mainz 1992) p. 14.

and it grounds every kind of understanding and every liturgical practice. It also grounds the very celebration itself, helping each and all to acquire the capacity to comprehend the euchological texts, the ritual dynamics, and their anthropological significance.

36. I think of the regular rhythm of our assemblies that come together to celebrate the Eucharist on the Lord's Day, Sunday after Sunday, Easter after Easter, at particular moments in the life of each single person and of the communities, in all the different ages of life. Ordained ministers carry out a pastoral action of the first importance when they take the baptised faithful by the hand to lead them into the repeated experience of the Paschal Mystery. Let us always remember that it is the Church, the Body of Christ, that is the celebrating subject and not just the priest. The kind of knowledge that comes from study is just the first step to be able to enter into the mystery celebrated. Obviously, to be able to lead their brothers and sisters, the ministers who preside in the assembly must know the way, know it from having studied it on the map of their theological studies but also from having frequented the liturgy in actual practice of an experience of living faith, nourished by prayer – and certainly not just as an obligation to be fulfilled. On the day of his ordination every priest hears the bishop say to him: "Understand what you will do, imitate what you will celebrate, and conform your life to the mystery of the Lord's Cross."[10]

37. Also the plan of studies for the Liturgy in seminaries must take account of the extraordinary capacity that the actual celebration has in itself to offer an organic and unified vision of all theological knowledge. Every discipline of theology, each from its own perspective, must show its own intimate connection with the Liturgy in light of which the unity of priestly formation is made clear and realised (cf. *Sacrosanctum Concilium*, n. 16). A

---

[10] *De Ordinatione Episcopi, Presbyterorum et Diaconorum* (1990) p. 95: "*Agnosce quod ages, imitare quod tractabis, et vitam tuam mysterio dominicæ crucis conforma*".

liturgical-sapiential plan of studies in the theological formation of seminaries would certainly have positive effects in pastoral action. There is no aspect of ecclesial life that does not find its summit and its source in the Liturgy. More than being the result of elaborate programmes, a comprehensive, organic, and integrated pastoral practice is the consequence of placing the Sunday Eucharist, the foundation of communion, at the centre of the life of the community. The theological understanding of the Liturgy does not in any way permit that these words be understood to mean to reduce everything to the aspect of worship. A celebration that does not evangelise is not authentic, just as a proclamation that does not lead to an encounter with the risen Lord in the celebration is not authentic. And then both of these, without the testimony of charity, are like sounding a noisy gong or a clanging cymbal (*1 Cor* 13:1).

38. For ministers as well as for all the baptised, liturgical formation in this first sense is not something that can be acquired once and for all. Since the gift of the mystery celebrated surpasses our capacity to know it, this effort certainly must accompany the permanent formation of everyone, with the humility of little ones, the attitude that opens up into wonder.

39. One final observation about seminaries: in addition to a programme of studies, they must also offer the possibility of experiencing a celebration that is not only exemplary from a ritual point of view, but also authentic and alive, which allows the living out of a true communion with God, that same communion towards which theological knowledge must tend. Only the action of the Spirit can bring to completion our knowledge of the mystery of God, for the mystery of God is not a question of something grasped mentally but a relationship that touches all of life. Such experience is fundamental so that, once seminarians become ordained ministers, they can accompany communities in the same journey of knowledge of the mystery of God, which is the mystery of love.

40. This last consideration brings us to reflection on the second sense that we can understand in the expression "liturgical formation." I refer to our being formed, each one according to his or her vocation, from participation in the liturgical celebration. Even the knowledge that comes from studies, of which I was just speaking, for it not to become a sort of rationalism, must serve to realise the formative action of the Liturgy itself in every believer in Christ.

41. From all that we have said about the nature of the Liturgy it becomes clear that knowledge of the mystery of Christ, the decisive question for our lives, does not consist in a mental assimilation of some idea but in real existential engagement with his person. In this sense, Liturgy is not about "knowledge," and its scope is not primarily pedagogical, even though it does have great pedagogical value (cf. *Sacrosanctum Concilium,* n. 33). Rather, Liturgy is about praise, about rendering thanks for the Passover of the Son whose power reaches our lives. The celebration concerns the reality of our being docile to the action of the Spirit who operates through it until Christ be formed in us (cf. *Gal* 4:19). The full extent of our formation is our conformation to Christ. I repeat: it does not have to do with an abstract mental process, but with becoming him. This is the purpose for which the Spirit is given, whose action is always and only to confect the Body of Christ. It is that way with the Eucharistic bread, and with every one of the baptised called to become always more and more that which was received as a gift in Baptism; namely, being a member of the Body of Christ. Leo the Great writes, "Our participation in the Body and Blood of Christ has no other end than to make us become that which we eat."[11]

---

[11] Leo Magnus, *Sermo LXIII: De Passione Domini III,* 7.

42. This existential engagement happens – in continuity with and consistent with the method of Incarnation – in a sacramental way. The Liturgy is done with things that are the exact opposite of spiritual abstractions: bread, wine, oil, water, fragrances, fire, ashes, rock, fabrics, colours, body, words, sounds, silences, gestures, space, movement, action, order, time, light. The whole of creation is a manifestation of the love of God, and from when that same love was manifested in its fulness in the cross of Jesus, all of creation was drawn towards it. It is the whole of creation that is assumed in order to be placed at the service of encounter with the Word: incarnate, crucified, dead, risen, ascended to the Father. It is as the prayer over the water at the baptismal font sings, but also the prayer over the oil for sacred chrism and the words for the presentation of the bread and wine – all fruit of the earth and work of human hands.

43. The Liturgy gives glory to God not because we can add something to the beauty of the inaccessible light within which God dwells (cf. *1 Ti* 6:16). Nor can we add to the perfection of the angelic song which resounds eternally through the heavenly places. The Liturgy gives glory to God because it allows us – here, on earth – to see God in the celebration of the mysteries, and in seeing him to draw life from his Passover. We, who were dead through our sins and have been made be alive again with Christ – we are the glory of God. By grace we have been saved (*Eph* 2:5). Irenaeus, the *doctor unitatis,* reminds us of this: "The glory of God is man alive, and the life of man consists in seeing God: if the revelation of God through the creation already gives life to all living beings on earth, how much more then is the manifestation of the Father through the Word the cause of life for those who see God."[12]

---

[12] Irenæus Lugdunensis, *Adversus hæreses IV,20,7.*

44. Guardini writes, "Here there is outlined the first task of the work of liturgical formation: man must become once again capable of symbols."[13] This is a responsibility for all, for ordained ministers and the faithful alike. The task is not easy because modern man has become illiterate, no longer able to read symbols; it is almost as if their existence is not even suspected. This happens also with the symbol of our body. Our body is a symbol because it is an intimate union of soul and body; it is the visibility of the spiritual soul in the corporeal order; and in this consists human uniqueness, the specificity of the person irreducible to any other form of living being. Our openness to the transcendent, to God, is constitutive of us. Not to recognise this leads us inevitably not only to a not knowing of God but also to not knowing ourselves. It is enough to look at the paradoxical way in which the body is treated, in one moment cared for in an almost obsessive way, inspired by the myth of eternal youth, and in another moment reducing the body to a materiality to which there is denied every dignity. The fact is that value cannot be given to the body starting only from the body itself. Every symbol is at the same time both powerful and fragile. If it is not respected, if it is not treated for what it is, it shatters, loses its force, becomes insignificant.

We no longer have the gaze of St Francis, who looked at the sun – which he called brother because so he felt it to be – and saw it *beautiful and radiant with great splendour*, and, full of wonder, he sang that it *bears a likeness of you, Most High One*.[14] To have lost the capacity to grasp the symbolic value of the body and of every creature renders the symbolic language of the Liturgy almost inaccessible to the modern mentality. And yet there can be no question of renouncing such language. It cannot be renounced because it is how the Holy Trinity chose

---

[13] R. Guardini, *Liturgische Bildung* (1923) in *Liturgie und liturgische Bildung* (Mainz 1992) p. 36.

[14] *Cantico delle Creature*, Fonti Francescane, p. 263; Eng. trans. Francis of Assisi, *Early Documents*, vol. I, 113.

to reach us through the flesh of the Word. It is rather a question of recovering the capacity to use and understand the symbols of the Liturgy. We must not lose hope because this dimension in us, as I have just said, is constitutive; and despite the evils of materialism and spiritualism – both of them negations of the unity of soul and body – it is always ready to re-emerge, as is every truth.

45. So, the question I want to pose is how can we become once again capable of symbols? How can we again know how to read them and be able to live them? We know well that the celebration of the sacraments, by the grace of God, is efficacious in itself (*ex opere operato*), but this does not guarantee the full engagement of people without an adequate way of their placing themselves in relation to the language of the celebration. A symbolic "reading" is not a mental knowledge, not the acquisition of concepts, but rather a living experience.

46. Above all we must reacquire confidence about creation. I mean to say that things – the sacraments "are made" of things – come from God. To him they are oriented, and by him they have been assumed, and assumed in a particular way in the Incarnation, so that they can become instruments of salvation, vehicles of the Spirit, channels of grace. In this it is clear how vast is the distance between this vision and either a materialistic or spiritualistic vision. If created things are such a fundamental, essential part of the sacramental action that brings about our salvation, then we must arrange ourselves in their presence with a fresh, non-superficial regard, respectful and grateful. From the very beginning, created things contain the seed of the sanctifying grace of the sacraments.

47. Still thinking about how the Liturgy forms us, another decisive question is the education necessary to be able to acquire the interior attitude that will let us use and understand liturgical symbols. Let me express it in a simple way. I have in mind parents, or even more, perhaps, grandparents, but also our pastors and catechists. Many of us learned the power of the gestures of the liturgy from them, as, for example, the sign of the cross, kneeling, the formulas of our faith. Perhaps we do not have an actual memory of such learning, but we can easily imagine the gesture of a larger hand taking the little hand of a child and accompanying it slowly in tracing across the body for the first time the sign of our salvation. Words accompany the movement, these also said slowly, almost as if wanting to take possession of every instant of the gesture, to take possession of the whole body: "In the name of the Father... and of the Son... and of the Holy Spirit.... Amen." And then the hand of the child is left alone, and it is watched repeating it all alone, with help ready nearby if need be. But that gesture is now consigned, like a habit that will grow with him, imparting to it a meaning that only the Spirit knows how. From that moment forward that gesture, its symbolic force, is ours, it belongs to us; or better said, we belong to it. It gives us form. We are formed by it. Not many discourses are needed here. It is not necessary to have understood everything in that gesture. What is needed is being small, both in consigning it and in receiving it. The rest is the work of the Spirit. In this way we are initiated into symbolic language. We cannot let ourselves be robbed of such richness. Growing up we will have more ways of being able to understand, but always on the condition of remaining little ones.

Ars celebrandi

48. One way of caring for and growing in a vital understanding of the symbols of the Liturgy is certainly the *ars celebrandi*, the art of celebrating. This expression also is subject to different interpretations. Its sense becomes clear if we refer to the theological sense of the Liturgy described in *Sacrosanctum Concilium* n. 7, to which I have already referred several times. The *ars celebrandi* cannot be reduced to only a rubrical mechanism, much less should it be thought of as imaginative – sometimes wild – creativity without rules. The rite is in itself a norm, and the norm is never an end in itself, but it is always at the service of a higher reality that it means to protect.

49. As in any art, the *ars celebrandi* requires different kinds of knowledge. First of all, it requires an understanding of the dynamism that unfolds through the Liturgy. The action of the celebration is the place in which, by means of memorial, the Paschal Mystery is made present so that the baptised, through their participation, can experience it in their own lives. Without this understanding, the celebration easily falls into a preoccupation with the exterior (more or less refined) or into a concern only for rubrics (more or less rigid).

Then, it is necessary to know how the Holy Spirit acts in every celebration. The art of celebrating must be in harmony with the action of the Spirit. Only in this way will it be free from the subjectivisms that are the fruit of individual tastes dominating. Only in this way will it be free from the invasion of cultural elements that are taken on without discernment and that have nothing to do with a correct understanding of inculturation.

Finally, it is necessary to understand the dynamics of symbolic language, its particular nature, its efficacy.

50. From these brief indications it should be clear that the art of celebration is not something that can be improvised. Like every art, it requires consistent application. For an artisan, technique is enough. But for an artist, in addition to technical knowledge, there has also to be inspiration, which is a positive form of possession. The true artist does not possess an art but rather is possessed by it. One does not learn the art of celebrating by frequenting a course in public speaking or in persuasive techniques of communication (I am not judging intentions, just observing effects). Every tool can be useful, but it must be at the service of the nature of the Liturgy and the action of the Holy Spirit. A diligent dedication to the celebration is required, allowing the celebration itself to convey to us its art. Guardini writes: "We must understand how deeply we remain entrenched in individualism and subjectivism, how unaccustomed we have become to the demands of the 'great', and how small the parameters of our religious living are. We must regain the sense for the 'great' style of praying, the will towards the existential in prayer too. The way to achieve this, though, is through discipline, through giving up weak sentimentality; through serious work, carried out in obedience to the Church, on our religious being and acting."[15] This is how the art of celebrating is learned.

51. Speaking of this theme we are inclined to think of it only in regards to ordained ministers carrying out the service of presiding. But in fact this is an attitude that all the baptised are called to live. I think of all the gestures and words that belong to the assembly: gathering, careful walking in procession, being seated, standing, kneeling, singing, being in silence, acclamations, looking, listening. There are many ways in which the assembly, *as one body* (*Ne* 8:1), participates in the celebration. Everybody doing together the same gesture, everyone speaking together in one voice – this transmits to each individual the energy of the entire

---

[15] R. Guardini, *Liturgische Bildung* (1923) in *Liturgie und liturgische Bildung* (Mainz 1992) p. 99.

assembly. It is a uniformity that not only does not deaden but, on the contrary, educates individual believers to discover the authentic uniqueness of their personalities not in individualistic attitudes but in the awareness of being one body. It is not a question of following a book of liturgical etiquette. It is, rather, a "discipline," – in the way that Guardini referred to – which, if observed authentically, forms us. These are gestures and words that place order within our interior world making us live certain feelings, attitudes, behaviours. They are not the explanation of an ideal that we seek to let inspire us, but they are instead an action that engages the body in its entirety, that is to say, in its being a unity of body and soul.

52. Among the ritual acts that belong to the whole assembly, silence occupies a place of absolute importance. Many times it is expressly prescribed in the rubrics. The entire Eucharistic celebration is immersed in the silence which precedes its beginning and which marks every moment of its ritual unfolding. In fact, it is present in the penitential act, after the invitation "Let us pray," in the Liturgy of the Word (before the readings, between the readings and after the homily), in the Eucharistic prayer, after communion.[16] Such silence is not an inner haven in which to hide oneself in some sort of intimate isolation, as if leaving the ritual form behind as a distraction. That kind of silence would contradict the essence itself of the celebration. Liturgical silence is something much more grand: it is a symbol of the presence and action of the Holy Spirit who animates the entire action of the celebration. For this reason it constitutes a point of arrival within a liturgical sequence. Precisely because it is a symbol of the Spirit, it has the power to express the Spirit's multifaceted action. In this way, going over again the moments I just mentioned, silence moves to sorrow for sin and the desire for conversion. It awakens a readiness to hear the Word and awakens prayer. It disposes us to adore the Body and Blood of

---

[16] Cf. *Institutio Generalis Missalis Romani* nn. 45; 51; 54-56; 66; 71; 84; 88; 271.

Christ. It suggests to each one, in the intimacy of communion, what the Spirit would effect in our lives to conform us to the Bread broken. For all these reasons we are called to enact with extreme care the symbolic gesture of silence. Through it the Spirit gives us shape, gives us form.

53. Every gesture and every word contains a precise action that is always new because it meets with an always new moment in our own lives. I will explain what I mean with a simple example. We kneel to ask pardon, to bend our pride, to hand over to God our tears, to beg his intervention, to thank him for a gift received. It is always the same gesture which in essence declares our own being small in the presence of God. Nevertheless, done in different moments of our lives, it moulds our inner depths and then thereafter shows itself externally in our relation with God and with our brothers and sisters. Also kneeling should be done with art, that is to say, with a full awareness of its symbolic sense and the need that we have of this gesture to express our way of being in the presence of the Lord. And if all this is true for this simple gesture, how much more will it be for the celebration of the Word? Ah, what art are we summoned to learn for the proclamation of the Word, for the hearing of it, for letting it inspire our prayer, for making it become our very life? All of this is worthy of utmost attention – not formal or merely exterior, but living and interior – so that every gesture and every word of the celebration, expressed with "art," forms the Christian personality of each individual and of the community.

54. If it is true that the *ars celebrandi* is required of the entire assembly that celebrates, it is likewise true that ordained ministers must have a very particular concern for it. In visiting Christian communities, I have noticed that their way of living the liturgical celebration is conditioned – for better or, unfortunately, for worse – by the way in which their pastor presides in the assembly. We could say that there are different

"models" of presiding. Here is a possible list of approaches, which even though opposed to each other, characterise a way of presiding that is certainly inadequate: rigid austerity or an exasperating creativity, a spiritualising mysticism or a practical functionalism, a rushed briskness or an overemphasised slowness, a sloppy carelessness or an excessive finickiness, a superabundant friendliness or priestly impassibility. Granted the wide range of these examples, I think that the inadequacy of these models of presiding have a common root: a heightened personalism of the celebrating style which at times expresses a poorly concealed mania to be the centre of attention. Often this becomes more evident when our celebrations are transmitted over the air or online, something not always opportune and that needs further reflection. Be sure you understand me: these are not the most widespread behaviours, but still, not infrequently assemblies suffer from being thus abused.

55. There would be much more to say about the importance of presiding and what care it requires. On different occasions I dwelt on the demanding duty of preaching the homily.[17] Here I limit myself to several other broad considerations, always wanting to reflect with you on how we are formed by the Liturgy. I think about the regular rhythm of Sunday Mass in our communities, and I address myself therefore to priests, but implicitly to all ordained ministers.

56. The priest lives his characteristic participation in the celebration in virtue of the gift received in the sacrament of Holy Orders, and this is expressed precisely in presiding. Like all the roles he is called to carry out, this is not primarily a duty assigned to him by the community but is rather a consequence of the outpouring of the Holy Spirit received in ordination which equips him for such a task. The priest also is formed by his presiding in the celebrating assembly.

---

[17] Cf. Apostolic Exhortation *Evangelii gaudium*, (24th November 2013) nn. 135-144.

57. For this service to be well done – indeed, with art! – it is of fundamental importance that the priest have a keen awareness of being, through God's mercy, a particular presence of the risen Lord. The ordained minister is himself one of the types of presence of the Lord which render the Christian assembly unique, different from any other assembly (cf. *Sacrosanctum Concilium,* n. 7). This fact gives "sacramental" weight (in the broad sense) to all the gestures and words of the one presiding. The assembly has the right to be able to feel in those gestures and words the desire that the Lord has, today as at the Last Supper, to eat the Passover with us. So, the risen Lord is in the leading role, and not our own immaturities, assuming roles and behaviours which are simply not appropriate. The priest himself should be overpowered by this desire for communion that the Lord has toward each person. It is as if he were placed in the middle between Jesus's burning heart of love and the heart of each of the faithful, which is the object of the Lord's love. To preside at Eucharist is to be plunged into the furnace of God's love. When we are given to understand this reality, or even just to intuit something of it, we certainly would no longer need a *Directory* that would impose the proper behaviour. If we have need of that, then it is because of *the hardness of our hearts*. The highest norm, and therefore the most demanding, is the reality itself of the Eucharistic celebration, which selects words, gestures, feelings that will make us understand whether or not our use of these is at the level of the reality they serve. It is obvious that this cannot be improvised. It is an art. It requires application on the part of the priest, an assiduous tending to the fire of the love of the Lord that he came to ignite on the earth (*Lk* 12:49).

58. When the first community broke bread in obedience to the Lord's command, it did so under the gaze of Mary who accompanied the first steps of the Church: "these all continued with one accord in prayer with the women and Mary the mother of Jesus" (*Ac* 1:14). The Virgin Mother "watches over" the gestures of her Son confided to the Apostles. As she protected the Word made flesh in her womb after receiving the words of the angel Gabriel, she protects once again in the womb of the Church those gestures that form the body of her Son. The priest, who repeats those gestures in virtue of the gift received in the sacrament of Holy Orders, is himself protected in the womb of the Virgin. Do we really need a rule here to tell us how we ought to act?

59. Having become instruments for igniting the fire of the Lord's love on the earth, protected in the womb of Mary, Virgin made Church (as St Francis sang of her), priests should allow the Holy Spirit to work on them, to bring to completion the work he began in them at their ordination. The action of the Spirit offers to them the possibility of exercising their ministry of presiding in the Eucharistic assembly with the fear of Peter, aware of being a sinner (*Lk* 5:1-11), with the powerful humility of the suffering servant (cf. *Is* 42ff), with the desire "to be eaten" by the people entrusted to them in the daily exercise of the ministry.

60. It is the celebration itself that educates the priest to this level and quality of presiding. It is not, I repeat, a mental adhesion, even if our whole mind as well as all our sensitivity must be engaged in it. So, the priest is formed by presiding over the words and by the gestures that the Liturgy places on his lips and in his hands. He is not seated on a throne[18] because the Lord reigns with the humility of one who serves. He does not rob attention from the centrality of the altar, *a sign of Christ,*

---

[18] Cf. *Institutio Generalis Missalis Romani* n. 310.

from whose pierced side flowed blood and water, by which were established the Sacraments of the Church and *the centre of our praise and thanksgiving.*[19]

Approaching the altar for the offering, the priest is educated in humility and contrition by the words, "With humble spirit and contrite heart may we be accepted by you, O Lord, and may our sacrifice in your sight this day be pleasing to you, Lord God."[20] He cannot rely on himself for the ministry confided to him because the Liturgy invites him to pray to be purified through the sign of water, when he says, "Wash me, O Lord, from my iniquity and cleanse me from my sin."[21]

The words which the Liturgy places on his lips have different contents which require specific tonalities. A true *ars dicendi* is required of the priest by the importance of such words. These give shape and form to his interior feelings, in one moment in supplication of the Father in the name of the assembly, in another in an exhortation addressed to the assembly, in another by acclamation in one voice with the entire assembly.

In the Eucharistic prayer – in which also all of the baptised participate by listening *with reverence and in silence* and intervening with the acclamations[22] (IGMR 78-79) – the one presiding has the strength, *in the name of the whole holy people,* to remember before the Father the offering of his Son in the Last Supper, so that that immense gift might be rendered newly present on the altar. In that offering he participates with the offering of himself. The priest cannot recount the Last Supper to the Father without himself becoming a participant in it. He cannot say, "Take this, all of you and eat of it, for

---

[19] *Prex dedicationis* in *Ordo dedicationis ecclesiæ et altaris* (1977) p. 102.

[20] *Missale Romanum* (2008) p. 515: "*In spiritu humilitatis et in animo contrito suscipiamur a te, Domine; et sic fiat sacrificium nostrum in conspectu tuo hodie, ut placeat tibi, Domine Deus*".

[21] *Missale Romanum* (2008) p. 515: "*Lava me, Domine, ab iniquitate mea, et a peccato meo munda me*".

[22] Cf. *Institutio Generalis Missalis Romani*, nn. 78-79.

this is my Body which will be given up for you," and not live the same desire to offer his own body, his own life, for the people entrusted to him. This is what happens in the exercise of his ministry.

From all this and from many other things the priest is continually formed by the action of the celebration.

***

61. In this letter I have wanted simply to share some reflections which most certainly do not exhaust the immense treasure of the celebration of the holy mysteries. I ask all the bishops, priests, and deacons, the formators in seminaries, the instructors in theological faculties and schools of theology, and all catechists to help the holy people of God to draw from what is the first wellspring of Christian spirituality. We are called continually to rediscover the richness of the general principles exposed in the first numbers of *Sacrosanctum Concilium,* grasping the intimate bond between this first of the Council's constitutions and all the others. For this reason we cannot go back to that ritual form which the Council fathers, *cum Petro et sub Petro,* felt the need to reform, approving, under the guidance of the Holy Spirit and following their conscience as pastors, the principles from which was born the reform. The holy pontiffs St Paul VI and St John Paul II, approving the reformed liturgical books *ex decreto Sacrosancti Œcumenici Concilii Vaticani II,* have guaranteed the fidelity of the reform of the Council. For this reason I wrote *Traditionis custodes,* so that the Church may lift up, in the variety of so many languages, one and the same prayer capable of expressing her unity.[23]

As I have already written, I intend that this unity be re-established in the whole Church of the Roman Rite.

62. I would like this letter to help us to rekindle our wonder for the beauty of the truth of the Christian celebration, to remind us of the necessity of an authentic liturgical formation, and to recognise the importance of an art of celebrating that is at the service of the truth of the Paschal Mystery and of the participation of all of the baptised in it, each one according to his or her vocation.

---

[23] Cf. Paulus VI, *Constitutio apostolica Missale Romanum* (3 Aprilis 1969) in *AAS* 61 (1969) 222.

All this richness is not far from us. It is in our churches, in our Christian feasts, in the centrality of the Lord's Day, in the power of the sacraments we celebrate. Christian life is a continual journey of growth. We are called to let ourselves be formed in joy and in communion.

63. For this I desire to leave you with yet a further indication to follow along our way. I invite you to rediscover the meaning of the *liturgical year* and of *the Lord's Day*. Both of these were also left us by the Council (cf. *Sacrosanctum Concilium*, nn. 102-111).

64. In the light of all that we have said above, we see that the liturgical year is for us the possibility of growing in our knowledge of the mystery of Christ, immersing our life in the mystery of his Death and Resurrection, awaiting his return in glory. This is a true ongoing formation. Our life is not a random chaotic series of events, one following the other. It is rather a precise itinerary which, from one annual celebration of the his Death and Resurrection to the next, conforms us to him, *as we await the blessed hope and the coming of our Saviour, Jesus Christ*.[24]

65. As the time made new by the mystery of his Death and Resurrection flows on, every eighth day the Church celebrates in the Lord's day the event of our salvation. Sunday, before being a precept, is a gift that God makes for his people; and for this reason the Church safeguards it with a precept. The Sunday celebration offers to the Christian community the possibility of being formed by the Eucharist. From Sunday to Sunday the word of the Risen Lord illuminates our existence, wanting to achieve in us the end for which it was sent (cf. *Is* 55:10-11). From Sunday to Sunday, communion in the Body and Blood of Christ wants to make also of our lives a sacrifice pleasing to the

---

[24] *Missale Romanum* (2008) p. 598: "...*exspectantes beatam spem et adventum Salvatoris nostri Iesu Christi*".

Father, in the fraternal communion of sharing, of hospitality, of service. From Sunday to Sunday, the energy of the Bread broken sustains us in announcing the Gospel in which the authenticity of our celebration shows itself.

Let us abandon our polemics to listen together to what the Spirit is saying to the Church. Let us safeguard our communion. Let us continue to be astonished at the beauty of the Liturgy. The Paschal Mystery has been given to us. Let us allow ourselves to be embraced by the desire that the Lord continues to have to eat his Passover with us. All this under the gaze of Mary, Mother of the Church.

Given in Rome, at St John Lateran, on 29th June, the Solemnity of Sts Peter and Paul, Apostles, in the year 2022, the tenth of my Pontificate.

Let everyone be struck with fear,
let the whole world tremble,
and let the heavens exult
when Christ, the Son of the living God,
is present on the altar in the hands of a priest!
O wonderful loftiness and stupendous dignity!
O sublime humility! O humble sublimity!
The Lord of the universe, God and the Son of God,
so humbles himself that for our salvation
he hides himself under an ordinary piece of bread!
Brothers, look at the humility of God,
and pour out your hearts before him!
Humble yourselves that you may be exalted by him!
Hold back nothing of yourselves for yourselves,
that he who gives himself totally to you
may receive you totally!

St Francis of Assisi
A Letter to the Entire Order II, 26-29